50 One Pot Wonders: Simplified Cooking

By: Kelly Johnson

Table of Contents

- Classic Chicken Pot Pie Skillet
- Hearty Beef and Vegetable Stew
- Creamy Tuscan Chicken Pasta
- Vegetarian Chickpea Curry
- Shrimp and Sausage Jambalaya
- Spinach and Mushroom Risotto
- Slow-Cooked BBQ Pulled Pork
- One-Pot Ratatouille
- Thai Coconut Chicken Soup
- Mexican Quinoa Skillet
- Lemon Herb Salmon and Rice
- Spaghetti Bolognese
- Sweet Potato and Black Bean Chili
- Honey Garlic Chicken Thighs
- Indian Butter Chicken
- Teriyaki Beef Stir-Fry
- Creamy Broccoli Cheddar Soup
- Moroccan Lentil Stew
- Mediterranean Chicken Orzo
- Loaded Baked Potato Soup
- Zucchini and Sausage Skillet
- Garlic Shrimp Alfredo
- Korean Beef Bulgogi Bowl
- Classic Beef Stroganoff
- Spinach Artichoke Pasta
- Savory Lamb Tagine
- Peanut Chicken Noodles
- Cajun Dirty Rice
- Creamy Tomato Basil Soup
- Smoky Three-Bean Chili
- Mushroom Stroganoff
- Lemon Dill Cod with Potatoes
- Chicken and Dumplings
- Green Curry Vegetables
- Stuffed Bell Pepper Casserole

- Pork and Cabbage Stir-Fry
- BBQ Chicken and Cornbread Casserole
- One-Pot Paella
- Spinach Feta Orzo
- Ham and Cheese Macaroni Bake
- Saffron Chicken and Rice
- Thai Red Curry with Tofu
- Creamy Chicken Wild Rice Soup
- Sweet and Sour Pork Stir-Fry
- Beef and Barley Soup
- Vegetable Lo Mein
- Seafood Gumbo
- Rustic Tuscan Bean Soup
- One-Pan Breakfast Hash
- Cheeseburger Casserole

Classic Chicken Pot Pie Skillet

Ingredients

- **2 cups cooked chicken**, shredded or diced
- **1 cup frozen mixed vegetables** (peas, carrots, and corn)
- **1/2 cup diced onion**
- **3 tablespoons unsalted butter**
- **3 tablespoons all-purpose flour**
- **2 cups chicken broth**
- **1/2 cup heavy cream**
- **1 teaspoon garlic powder**
- **1 teaspoon dried thyme**
- **Salt and pepper**, to taste
- **1 pre-made pie crust**
- **1 egg**, beaten (for egg wash)

Instructions

1. **Preheat Oven:** Preheat your oven to 400°F (200°C).
2. **Cook Vegetables:** In a large oven-safe skillet, melt butter over medium heat. Add diced onion and sauté for 2-3 minutes until softened. Stir in the frozen vegetables and cook for another 2 minutes.
3. **Make the Gravy:** Sprinkle the flour over the vegetables and stir until evenly coated. Cook for 1-2 minutes to remove the raw flour taste. Gradually whisk in the chicken broth, ensuring no lumps. Simmer for 5 minutes until the mixture thickens.
4. **Add Chicken and Seasoning:** Stir in the cooked chicken, heavy cream, garlic powder, thyme, salt, and pepper. Let the filling simmer for 3-4 minutes, then remove the skillet from heat.
5. **Prepare the Pie Crust:** Roll out the pie crust and place it over the skillet, trimming any excess. Tuck the edges slightly inward around the rim of the skillet. Cut small slits in the center to allow steam to escape.
6. **Brush with Egg Wash:** Lightly brush the pie crust with the beaten egg for a golden finish.
7. **Bake:** Place the skillet in the preheated oven and bake for 20-25 minutes, or until the crust is golden brown.
8. **Serve:** Remove from the oven and let cool for 5-10 minutes before serving. Scoop portions directly from the skillet and enjoy!

Hearty Beef and Vegetable Stew

Ingredients:

- **1 lb beef stew meat**, cubed
- **3 tablespoons olive oil**
- **4 cups beef broth**
- **2 carrots**, peeled and sliced
- **2 potatoes**, cubed
- **1 onion**, diced
- **2 celery stalks**, chopped
- **2 garlic cloves**, minced
- **1 teaspoon dried thyme**
- **1 teaspoon dried rosemary**
- **Salt and pepper**, to taste
- **1 cup frozen peas**

Instructions:

1. Heat olive oil in a large pot over medium heat. Brown the beef stew meat in batches. Set aside.
2. In the same pot, sauté the onion, garlic, carrots, and celery until softened, about 5 minutes.
3. Add the beef back into the pot along with the potatoes, thyme, rosemary, salt, and pepper. Pour in the beef broth and bring to a simmer.
4. Reduce the heat to low and cook for 1 to 1.5 hours, until the beef is tender and the vegetables are cooked through.
5. Stir in the peas and cook for another 5 minutes before serving.

Creamy Tuscan Chicken Pasta

Ingredients:

- **2 chicken breasts**, sliced
- **2 tablespoons olive oil**
- **3 garlic cloves**, minced
- **1 cup sun-dried tomatoes**, chopped
- **1 cup heavy cream**
- **1/2 cup chicken broth**
- **8 oz pasta** (penne or fettuccine)
- **1 cup spinach**, chopped
- **1/4 cup grated Parmesan cheese**
- **Salt and pepper**, to taste

Instructions:

1. Heat olive oil in a large skillet over medium heat. Cook the chicken until browned and cooked through, about 6-8 minutes.
2. Remove the chicken and set aside. In the same skillet, add garlic and sun-dried tomatoes, cooking for 1 minute.
3. Add the heavy cream, chicken broth, and Parmesan. Stir to combine and bring to a simmer.
4. Meanwhile, cook the pasta according to package instructions. Drain and add to the skillet.
5. Add the spinach and cooked chicken, stirring to combine. Cook for 2-3 minutes until everything is heated through. Season with salt and pepper.

Vegetarian Chickpea Curry

Ingredients:

- **1 can chickpeas**, drained and rinsed
- **1 onion**, diced
- **2 garlic cloves**, minced
- **1 tablespoon ginger**, minced
- **1 can diced tomatoes**
- **1 cup coconut milk**
- **1 tablespoon curry powder**
- **1 teaspoon ground cumin**
- **1 teaspoon turmeric**
- **Salt and pepper**, to taste
- **1 cup spinach**, chopped
- **1 tablespoon olive oil**

Instructions:

1. Heat olive oil in a large pot over medium heat. Sauté the onion, garlic, and ginger until softened, about 5 minutes.
2. Stir in the curry powder, cumin, turmeric, salt, and pepper, cooking for 1 minute.
3. Add the tomatoes, coconut milk, and chickpeas. Bring to a simmer and cook for 10-15 minutes.
4. Stir in the spinach and cook until wilted. Serve with rice or naan.

Shrimp and Sausage Jambalaya

Ingredients:

- **1 lb shrimp**, peeled and deveined
- **1 lb sausage**, sliced (andouille or smoked sausage)
- **1 onion**, diced
- **1 bell pepper**, diced
- **2 celery stalks**, chopped
- **2 garlic cloves**, minced
- **1 can diced tomatoes**
- **2 cups chicken broth**
- **1 cup long-grain rice**
- **1 teaspoon paprika**
- **1/2 teaspoon cayenne pepper**
- **Salt and pepper**, to taste
- **2 tablespoons olive oil**

Instructions:

1. Heat olive oil in a large skillet or pot. Brown the sausage slices and remove. Set aside.
2. In the same pot, sauté the onion, bell pepper, celery, and garlic for 5 minutes.
3. Stir in the rice, paprika, cayenne, and tomatoes. Add the chicken broth and bring to a simmer.
4. Cover and cook for 20-25 minutes, until the rice is tender and the liquid is absorbed.
5. Stir in the shrimp and sausage. Cook for another 5 minutes until the shrimp is cooked through.

Spinach and Mushroom Risotto

Ingredients:

- **1 cup Arborio rice**
- **1 tablespoon olive oil**
- **1 small onion**, diced
- **2 garlic cloves**, minced
- **2 cups mushrooms**, sliced
- **4 cups chicken or vegetable broth**, warmed
- **1/2 cup dry white wine**
- **2 cups spinach**, chopped
- **1/2 cup Parmesan cheese**
- **Salt and pepper**, to taste

Instructions:

1. In a large skillet, heat olive oil over medium heat. Sauté the onion, garlic, and mushrooms for about 5 minutes until the mushrooms soften.
2. Stir in the Arborio rice and cook for 1-2 minutes, allowing the rice to lightly toast.
3. Add the white wine and cook, stirring, until absorbed.
4. Gradually add the broth, one cup at a time, stirring frequently. Wait until the liquid is absorbed before adding more.
5. When the rice is tender and creamy (about 20 minutes), stir in the spinach and Parmesan. Season with salt and pepper.

Slow-Cooked BBQ Pulled Pork

Ingredients:

- 3-4 lb pork shoulder
- 1 cup BBQ sauce
- 1/4 cup apple cider vinegar
- 1 tablespoon paprika
- 1 teaspoon garlic powder
- 1 teaspoon onion powder
- 1 teaspoon chili powder
- **Salt and pepper**, to taste

Instructions:

1. In a small bowl, combine the paprika, garlic powder, onion powder, chili powder, salt, and pepper. Rub the seasoning onto the pork shoulder.
2. Place the pork in a slow cooker. Mix the BBQ sauce and apple cider vinegar and pour over the pork.
3. Cook on low for 8 hours or high for 4 hours, until the pork is tender and easily shredded.
4. Shred the pork with two forks and mix with the sauce. Serve on buns or with your favorite sides.

One-Pot Ratatouille

Ingredients:

- **1 zucchini**, diced
- **1 eggplant**, diced
- **1 bell pepper**, diced
- **1 onion**, diced
- **2 garlic cloves**, minced
- **1 can diced tomatoes**
- **1 tablespoon olive oil**
- **1 teaspoon dried oregano**
- **1 teaspoon dried thyme**
- **Salt and pepper**, to taste

Instructions:

1. Heat olive oil in a large pot. Sauté the onion, garlic, zucchini, eggplant, and bell pepper for 5-7 minutes until softened.
2. Add the diced tomatoes, oregano, thyme, salt, and pepper. Bring to a simmer.
3. Cover and cook for 20 minutes, stirring occasionally, until the vegetables are tender. Serve with bread or over rice.

Thai Coconut Chicken Soup

Ingredients:

- **2 chicken breasts**, thinly sliced
- **1 can coconut milk**
- **4 cups chicken broth**
- **1 tablespoon ginger**, minced
- **2 garlic cloves**, minced
- **2 tablespoons lime juice**
- **2 tablespoons fish sauce**
- **1-2 Thai bird's eye chilies**, sliced (optional)
- **1 cup mushrooms**, sliced
- **1/2 cup cilantro**, chopped
- **1 tablespoon olive oil**

Instructions:

1. Heat olive oil in a large pot over medium heat. Add the ginger and garlic, cooking for 1-2 minutes until fragrant.
2. Pour in the chicken broth and coconut milk. Bring to a simmer.
3. Add the chicken, mushrooms, fish sauce, lime juice, and chilies (if using). Cook for 10 minutes until the chicken is cooked through.
4. Stir in the cilantro and serve with additional lime wedges.

Mexican Quinoa Skillet

Ingredients:

- **1 cup quinoa**, rinsed
- **1 can black beans**, drained and rinsed
- **1 cup corn kernels**
- **1 bell pepper**, diced
- **1 onion**, diced
- **1 teaspoon cumin**
- **1 teaspoon chili powder**
- **1/2 cup salsa**
- **1 cup chicken broth**
- **1/4 cup fresh cilantro**, chopped
- **Lime wedges**, for serving

Instructions:

1. In a large skillet, sauté the onion and bell pepper in a bit of olive oil until softened, about 5 minutes.
2. Add the quinoa, cumin, and chili powder. Stir to combine.
3. Pour in the chicken broth and salsa, bring to a simmer. Cover and cook for 15 minutes.
4. Stir in the black beans, corn, and cilantro. Cook for an additional 5 minutes. Serve with lime wedges.

Lemon Herb Salmon and Rice

Ingredients:

- **4 salmon fillets**
- **2 tablespoons olive oil**
- **1 tablespoon lemon juice**
- **2 teaspoons garlic powder**
- **1 teaspoon dried thyme**
- **1 teaspoon dried rosemary**
- **Salt and pepper**, to taste
- **1 cup jasmine or basmati rice**
- **2 cups water or chicken broth**
- **1 tablespoon butter**
- **1 tablespoon fresh parsley**, chopped

Instructions:

1. Preheat the oven to 400°F (200°C).
2. In a small bowl, mix together olive oil, lemon juice, garlic powder, thyme, rosemary, salt, and pepper.
3. Place the salmon fillets on a baking sheet lined with parchment paper. Brush the salmon with the lemon herb mixture.
4. Bake the salmon for 12-15 minutes, until cooked through and flaky.
5. Meanwhile, cook the rice by combining it with water or chicken broth in a medium saucepan. Bring to a boil, then reduce heat, cover, and simmer for 15-18 minutes.
6. Fluff the rice with a fork, then stir in the butter.
7. Serve the salmon over the rice, garnished with fresh parsley.

Spaghetti Bolognese

Ingredients:

- **1 lb ground beef or pork**
- **1 onion**, chopped
- **2 garlic cloves**, minced
- **1 carrot**, diced
- **1 celery stalk**, chopped
- **1 can diced tomatoes**
- **1/2 cup tomato paste**
- **1/4 cup red wine** (optional)
- **2 teaspoons dried oregano**
- **1 teaspoon dried basil**
- **Salt and pepper**, to taste
- **1 lb spaghetti**
- **Parmesan cheese**, for serving

Instructions:

1. Heat a large skillet over medium heat. Add the ground meat and cook until browned. Remove excess fat.
2. Add the onion, garlic, carrot, and celery to the skillet, cooking for about 5 minutes until softened.
3. Stir in the diced tomatoes, tomato paste, red wine (if using), oregano, basil, salt, and pepper. Simmer for 20-30 minutes, stirring occasionally.
4. Meanwhile, cook the spaghetti according to package instructions. Drain and set aside.
5. Serve the Bolognese sauce over the spaghetti, topped with grated Parmesan.

Sweet Potato and Black Bean Chili

Ingredients:

- **2 large sweet potatoes**, peeled and diced
- **1 can black beans**, drained and rinsed
- **1 onion**, chopped
- **2 garlic cloves**, minced
- **1 bell pepper**, diced
- **1 can diced tomatoes**
- **1 tablespoon chili powder**
- **1 teaspoon cumin**
- **1/2 teaspoon smoked paprika**
- **Salt and pepper**, to taste
- **2 cups vegetable broth**
- **1 tablespoon olive oil**

Instructions:

1. Heat olive oil in a large pot over medium heat. Sauté the onion, garlic, and bell pepper for 5 minutes until softened.
2. Add the diced sweet potatoes, black beans, diced tomatoes, chili powder, cumin, smoked paprika, salt, and pepper. Stir to combine.
3. Pour in the vegetable broth and bring to a simmer. Cover and cook for 25-30 minutes, until the sweet potatoes are tender.
4. Adjust seasoning and serve hot. Optional toppings include sour cream or shredded cheese.

Honey Garlic Chicken Thighs

Ingredients:

- 4 bone-in, skin-on chicken thighs
- 2 tablespoons honey
- 3 tablespoons soy sauce
- 3 garlic cloves, minced
- 1 tablespoon olive oil
- 1 teaspoon dried thyme
- Salt and pepper, to taste
- 1 tablespoon fresh parsley, chopped

Instructions:

1. Preheat the oven to 400°F (200°C).
2. In a small bowl, whisk together honey, soy sauce, garlic, olive oil, thyme, salt, and pepper.
3. Place the chicken thighs on a baking sheet and pour the honey garlic mixture over them.
4. Bake for 35-40 minutes, or until the chicken is cooked through and the skin is crispy.
5. Garnish with fresh parsley before serving.

Indian Butter Chicken

Ingredients:

- **1 lb boneless, skinless chicken breasts**, cubed
- **1 tablespoon butter**
- **1 onion**, diced
- **3 garlic cloves**, minced
- **1 tablespoon ginger**, minced
- **1 tablespoon garam masala**
- **1 teaspoon ground cumin**
- **1 teaspoon ground coriander**
- **1 teaspoon chili powder**
- **1/2 teaspoon turmeric**
- **1 can tomato puree**
- **1/2 cup heavy cream**
- **Salt and pepper**, to taste
- **2 tablespoons fresh cilantro**, chopped

Instructions:

1. Heat butter in a large skillet over medium heat. Cook the chicken pieces until browned, about 6-8 minutes. Remove and set aside.
2. In the same skillet, sauté the onion, garlic, and ginger until softened, about 5 minutes.
3. Stir in the garam masala, cumin, coriander, chili powder, and turmeric, cooking for 1 minute.
4. Add the tomato puree, heavy cream, salt, and pepper. Stir to combine and simmer for 10-15 minutes.
5. Return the chicken to the skillet, simmering for another 5-7 minutes until cooked through.
6. Garnish with cilantro and serve with naan or rice.

Teriyaki Beef Stir-Fry

Ingredients:

- **1 lb beef sirloin or flank steak**, thinly sliced
- **1 tablespoon olive oil**
- **2 bell peppers**, sliced
- **1 onion**, sliced
- **2 cups broccoli florets**
- **1/2 cup teriyaki sauce**
- **2 tablespoons soy sauce**
- **1 tablespoon sesame oil**
- **1 tablespoon cornstarch (optional, for thickening)**
- **1 tablespoon sesame seeds**, for garnish

Instructions:

1. Heat olive oil in a large skillet or wok over medium-high heat. Add the beef and cook until browned, about 5-6 minutes. Remove and set aside.
2. In the same skillet, add the bell peppers, onion, and broccoli. Stir-fry for 3-4 minutes until tender-crisp.
3. In a small bowl, mix the teriyaki sauce, soy sauce, sesame oil, and cornstarch (if using). Pour the sauce over the vegetables and stir to coat.
4. Add the beef back to the skillet and cook for an additional 2 minutes, until heated through and the sauce has thickened.
5. Garnish with sesame seeds and serve hot with rice.

Creamy Broccoli Cheddar Soup

Ingredients:

- **1 tablespoon butter**
- **1 onion**, diced
- **2 garlic cloves**, minced
- **4 cups broccoli florets**
- **3 cups chicken broth**
- **1 cup milk**
- **1 cup shredded cheddar cheese**
- **Salt and pepper**, to taste
- **1 tablespoon flour** (optional, for thickening)

Instructions:

1. Melt butter in a large pot over medium heat. Sauté the onion and garlic for 5 minutes, until softened.
2. Add the broccoli and chicken broth, bringing to a boil. Reduce heat and simmer for 10-15 minutes, until the broccoli is tender.
3. Use an immersion blender to puree the soup (or transfer in batches to a regular blender). For a thicker soup, stir in 1 tablespoon of flour.
4. Return the soup to heat and stir in the milk and shredded cheddar cheese. Continue cooking until the cheese is melted and the soup is creamy.
5. Season with salt and pepper and serve warm.

Moroccan Lentil Stew

Ingredients:

- **1 cup dried lentils**, rinsed
- **1 onion**, diced
- **2 garlic cloves**, minced
- **2 carrots**, diced
- **1 celery stalk**, chopped
- **1 can diced tomatoes**
- **4 cups vegetable broth**
- **1 teaspoon cumin**
- **1 teaspoon coriander**
- **1/2 teaspoon cinnamon**
- **1/2 teaspoon turmeric**
- **Salt and pepper**, to taste
- **1 tablespoon olive oil**
- **1 tablespoon fresh cilantro**, chopped

Instructions:

1. Heat olive oil in a large pot over medium heat. Add the onion, garlic, carrots, and celery. Sauté for 5 minutes until softened.
2. Stir in the cumin, coriander, cinnamon, turmeric, salt, and pepper. Cook for 1 minute to toast the spices.
3. Add the lentils, diced tomatoes, and vegetable broth. Bring to a boil, then reduce heat and simmer for 30-40 minutes, until the lentils are tender.
4. Garnish with fresh cilantro before serving.

Mediterranean Chicken Orzo

Ingredients:

- **4 chicken breasts**, boneless and skinless
- **1 tablespoon olive oil**
- **1 cup orzo pasta**
- **1 cup cherry tomatoes**, halved
- **1 cucumber**, diced
- **1/4 cup Kalamata olives**, chopped
- **1/4 cup feta cheese**, crumbled
- **2 tablespoons fresh parsley**, chopped
- **1 tablespoon lemon juice**
- **1 teaspoon dried oregano**
- **Salt and pepper**, to taste

Instructions:

1. Heat olive oil in a large skillet over medium heat. Cook the chicken breasts for 6-7 minutes per side until fully cooked. Remove from heat and let rest before slicing.
2. Cook the orzo according to package instructions. Drain and set aside.
3. In a large bowl, combine the cooked orzo, cherry tomatoes, cucumber, olives, feta, parsley, lemon juice, oregano, salt, and pepper.
4. Serve the orzo salad topped with sliced chicken. Enjoy!

Loaded Baked Potato Soup

Ingredients:

- **4 large russet potatoes**, peeled and diced
- **1 tablespoon butter**
- **1 onion**, diced
- **2 garlic cloves**, minced
- **4 cups chicken broth**
- **1 cup heavy cream**
- **1 cup shredded cheddar cheese**
- **1/2 cup sour cream**
- **Salt and pepper**, to taste
- **4 slices cooked bacon**, crumbled
- **Green onions**, chopped for garnish

Instructions:

1. In a large pot, melt butter over medium heat. Add the onion and garlic, cooking for 3-4 minutes until softened.
2. Add the diced potatoes and chicken broth to the pot. Bring to a boil, then reduce heat and simmer for 15-20 minutes until the potatoes are tender.
3. Use a potato masher to mash the potatoes, leaving some chunks for texture.
4. Stir in the heavy cream, cheddar cheese, and sour cream. Cook for 5-10 minutes, stirring occasionally, until the soup is creamy and thickened.
5. Season with salt and pepper, then serve topped with crumbled bacon and green onions.

Zucchini and Sausage Skillet

Ingredients:

- **1 lb Italian sausage**, removed from casing
- **2 zucchinis**, sliced
- **1 onion**, diced
- **2 garlic cloves**, minced
- **1 teaspoon dried oregano**
- **1/2 teaspoon red pepper flakes** (optional)
- **Salt and pepper**, to taste
- **2 tablespoons olive oil**
- **1 tablespoon fresh basil**, chopped for garnish

Instructions:

1. Heat olive oil in a large skillet over medium heat. Add the sausage and cook, breaking it apart with a spoon, until browned and cooked through.
2. Add the diced onion and garlic, cooking for 3-4 minutes until softened.
3. Stir in the zucchini, oregano, red pepper flakes, salt, and pepper. Cook for another 5-7 minutes, until the zucchini is tender.
4. Garnish with fresh basil before serving.

Garlic Shrimp Alfredo

Ingredients:

- **1 lb shrimp**, peeled and deveined
- **1 tablespoon olive oil**
- **3 garlic cloves**, minced
- **1 cup heavy cream**
- **1/2 cup grated Parmesan cheese**
- **1 lb fettuccine pasta**
- **Salt and pepper**, to taste
- **1 tablespoon fresh parsley**, chopped for garnish

Instructions:

1. Cook the fettuccine pasta according to package instructions. Drain and set aside.
2. In a large skillet, heat olive oil over medium heat. Add the shrimp and cook for 2-3 minutes per side, until pink and opaque. Remove and set aside.
3. In the same skillet, add the garlic and sauté for 1 minute until fragrant.
4. Stir in the heavy cream and Parmesan cheese, cooking for 2-3 minutes until the sauce thickens.
5. Add the cooked pasta and shrimp to the skillet, tossing to coat in the sauce. Season with salt and pepper.
6. Garnish with fresh parsley before serving.

Korean Beef Bulgogi Bowl

Ingredients:

- **1 lb flank steak**, thinly sliced
- **1/4 cup soy sauce**
- **2 tablespoons brown sugar**
- **2 tablespoons sesame oil**
- **3 garlic cloves**, minced
- **1 tablespoon grated ginger**
- **1 tablespoon rice vinegar**
- **1 teaspoon gochujang (Korean chili paste)** (optional)
- **2 tablespoons sesame seeds**
- **2 green onions**, chopped for garnish
- **2 cups cooked rice**, for serving

Instructions:

1. In a bowl, whisk together the soy sauce, brown sugar, sesame oil, garlic, ginger, rice vinegar, and gochujang (if using).
2. Add the sliced beef to the marinade and toss to coat. Let marinate for 30 minutes to 1 hour.
3. Heat a skillet over medium-high heat and cook the beef for 3-4 minutes, until browned and cooked through.
4. Serve the beef over cooked rice, garnished with sesame seeds and green onions.

Classic Beef Stroganoff

Ingredients:

- **1 lb beef sirloin or tenderloin**, sliced thin
- **1 tablespoon olive oil**
- **1 onion**, chopped
- **3 garlic cloves**, minced
- **8 oz mushrooms**, sliced
- **1 cup beef broth**
- **1 tablespoon Dijon mustard**
- **1/2 cup sour cream**
- **Salt and pepper**, to taste
- **Egg noodles**, for serving
- **Fresh parsley**, chopped for garnish

Instructions:

1. Heat olive oil in a large skillet over medium-high heat. Add the beef and cook until browned, about 3-4 minutes per side. Remove the beef and set aside.
2. In the same skillet, add the onion, garlic, and mushrooms. Cook for 5-7 minutes until the vegetables are softened.
3. Stir in the beef broth and Dijon mustard, scraping any browned bits from the bottom of the skillet. Bring to a simmer and cook for 5 minutes.
4. Stir in the sour cream and return the beef to the skillet. Cook for another 2-3 minutes until heated through.
5. Serve over egg noodles, garnished with fresh parsley.

Spinach Artichoke Pasta

Ingredients:

- **8 oz pasta**, such as penne or rigatoni
- **2 tablespoons olive oil**
- **3 garlic cloves**, minced
- **1 can artichoke hearts**, drained and chopped
- **4 cups fresh spinach**, chopped
- **1 cup heavy cream**
- **1/2 cup grated Parmesan cheese**
- **Salt and pepper**, to taste
- **1/4 cup shredded mozzarella cheese**

Instructions:

1. Cook the pasta according to package instructions. Drain and set aside.
2. Heat olive oil in a large skillet over medium heat. Add the garlic and sauté for 1 minute.
3. Stir in the artichokes and spinach, cooking until the spinach wilts.
4. Add the heavy cream, Parmesan cheese, salt, and pepper. Simmer for 5 minutes until the sauce thickens.
5. Toss the cooked pasta in the sauce, then top with mozzarella cheese. Serve hot.

Savory Lamb Tagine

Ingredients:

- **1 lb lamb stew meat**, cut into chunks
- **2 tablespoons olive oil**
- **1 onion**, chopped
- **3 garlic cloves**, minced
- **1 tablespoon ground cumin**
- **1 tablespoon ground coriander**
- **1 teaspoon ground cinnamon**
- **1/2 teaspoon ground turmeric**
- **1 can diced tomatoes**
- **2 cups vegetable broth**
- **1/4 cup dried apricots**, chopped
- **1/4 cup almonds**, toasted for garnish
- **Fresh cilantro**, chopped for garnish
- **Couscous**, for serving

Instructions:

1. Heat olive oil in a large Dutch oven or tagine over medium heat. Brown the lamb in batches, then set aside.
2. In the same pot, sauté the onion and garlic until softened.
3. Stir in the cumin, coriander, cinnamon, and turmeric. Cook for 1 minute to toast the spices.
4. Return the lamb to the pot along with the diced tomatoes, vegetable broth, and apricots. Bring to a simmer, then cover and cook for 1.5 to 2 hours, until the lamb is tender.
5. Serve the tagine with couscous, garnished with toasted almonds and cilantro.

Peanut Chicken Noodles

Ingredients:

- **2 chicken breasts**, cooked and shredded
- **8 oz rice noodles** (or spaghetti)
- **1 tablespoon olive oil**
- **1/4 cup peanut butter**
- **2 tablespoons soy sauce**
- **2 tablespoons honey**
- **2 tablespoons rice vinegar**
- **1 teaspoon sesame oil**
- **1/4 cup water**
- **1/4 teaspoon red pepper flakes** (optional)
- **Chopped peanuts** for garnish
- **Green onions**, chopped for garnish

Instructions:

1. Cook the noodles according to package instructions. Drain and set aside.
2. In a small bowl, whisk together the peanut butter, soy sauce, honey, rice vinegar, sesame oil, water, and red pepper flakes (if using).
3. Heat olive oil in a skillet over medium heat. Add the shredded chicken and cook for 2-3 minutes until warmed through.
4. Add the cooked noodles and peanut sauce, tossing to coat. Heat for another 2-3 minutes.
5. Serve garnished with chopped peanuts and green onions.

Cajun Dirty Rice

Ingredients:

- **1 lb ground pork or sausage**
- **1 onion**, chopped
- **1 bell pepper**, chopped
- **2 celery stalks**, chopped
- **3 garlic cloves**, minced
- **2 cups long-grain white rice**
- **4 cups chicken broth**
- **1 tablespoon Cajun seasoning**
- **1/2 teaspoon dried thyme**
- **Salt and pepper**, to taste
- **2 green onions**, chopped for garnish

Instructions:

1. In a large skillet, cook the ground pork or sausage over medium heat, breaking it apart as it cooks.
2. Add the onion, bell pepper, celery, and garlic. Cook for 5-7 minutes until softened.
3. Stir in the rice, chicken broth, Cajun seasoning, thyme, salt, and pepper. Bring to a simmer, then cover and cook for 20-25 minutes until the rice is cooked.
4. Garnish with green onions and serve hot.

Creamy Tomato Basil Soup

Ingredients:

- 2 tablespoons olive oil
- 1 onion, chopped
- 3 garlic cloves, minced
- 2 cans (14.5 oz each) diced tomatoes
- 2 cups vegetable broth
- 1/2 teaspoon dried oregano
- 1/2 teaspoon sugar
- 1 cup heavy cream
- 1/4 cup fresh basil, chopped
- Salt and pepper, to taste

Instructions:

1. Heat olive oil in a large pot over medium heat. Add the onion and garlic, sautéing for 3-4 minutes until softened.
2. Stir in the diced tomatoes, vegetable broth, oregano, and sugar. Bring to a simmer and cook for 10-15 minutes to allow the flavors to meld.
3. Use an immersion blender to blend the soup until smooth (or transfer to a blender in batches).
4. Stir in the heavy cream and fresh basil, and cook for another 5 minutes.
5. Season with salt and pepper before serving.

Smoky Three-Bean Chili

Ingredients:

- **1 tablespoon olive oil**
- **1 onion**, chopped
- **2 garlic cloves**, minced
- **1 bell pepper**, chopped
- **1 can (15 oz) kidney beans**, drained and rinsed
- **1 can (15 oz) black beans**, drained and rinsed
- **1 can (15 oz) pinto beans**, drained and rinsed
- **1 can (14.5 oz) diced tomatoes**
- **1/4 cup tomato paste**
- **1 tablespoon chili powder**
- **1 teaspoon smoked paprika**
- **1 teaspoon cumin**
- **1/2 teaspoon red pepper flakes** (optional)
- **2 cups vegetable broth**
- **Salt and pepper**, to taste

Instructions:

1. Heat olive oil in a large pot over medium heat. Add the onion, garlic, and bell pepper, sautéing for 5-7 minutes until softened.
2. Stir in the beans, diced tomatoes, tomato paste, chili powder, smoked paprika, cumin, and red pepper flakes (if using).
3. Add the vegetable broth, bring to a simmer, and cook for 25-30 minutes, stirring occasionally.
4. Season with salt and pepper to taste, and serve hot.

Mushroom Stroganoff

Ingredients:

- **2 tablespoons butter**
- **1 onion**, chopped
- **3 garlic cloves**, minced
- **16 oz mushrooms**, sliced
- **1 teaspoon dried thyme**
- **1 tablespoon flour**
- **1 cup vegetable broth**
- **1 cup sour cream**
- **Salt and pepper**, to taste
- **Egg noodles**, for serving
- **Fresh parsley**, chopped for garnish

Instructions:

1. Heat butter in a large skillet over medium heat. Add the onion and garlic, sautéing for 3-4 minutes until softened.
2. Add the mushrooms and thyme, cooking for 7-10 minutes until the mushrooms release their moisture and become tender.
3. Stir in the flour and cook for 1 minute. Gradually add the vegetable broth, stirring to combine, and simmer for 5 minutes.
4. Remove from heat and stir in the sour cream. Season with salt and pepper.
5. Serve the mushroom stroganoff over cooked egg noodles, garnished with fresh parsley.

Lemon Dill Cod with Potatoes

Ingredients:

- **4 cod fillets**
- **4 medium potatoes**, diced
- **2 tablespoons olive oil**
- **1 teaspoon garlic powder**
- **1 teaspoon dried dill**
- **Juice and zest of 1 lemon**
- **Salt and pepper**, to taste
- **Fresh dill**, chopped for garnish

Instructions:

1. Preheat the oven to 400°F (200°C). Toss the diced potatoes with 1 tablespoon of olive oil, garlic powder, dill, salt, and pepper. Spread on a baking sheet and bake for 20-25 minutes until tender.
2. In a separate pan, heat the remaining olive oil over medium heat. Season the cod fillets with salt, pepper, and half of the lemon zest.
3. Cook the cod for 3-4 minutes per side, until golden and flaky.
4. Serve the cod with roasted potatoes, drizzled with lemon juice, and garnished with fresh dill and the remaining lemon zest.

Chicken and Dumplings

Ingredients:

- **1 lb chicken breasts**, cooked and shredded
- **2 tablespoons butter**
- **1 onion**, chopped
- **2 celery stalks**, chopped
- **2 carrots**, chopped
- **3 garlic cloves**, minced
- **1/2 teaspoon thyme**
- **1 teaspoon dried parsley**
- **4 cups chicken broth**
- **1 cup heavy cream**
- **2 cups flour**
- **2 teaspoons baking powder**
- **1/2 teaspoon salt**
- **1/2 cup milk**

Instructions:

1. In a large pot, melt butter over medium heat. Add the onion, celery, and carrots, cooking for 5-7 minutes until softened.
2. Stir in the garlic, thyme, and parsley, cooking for another 1-2 minutes. Add the chicken broth and heavy cream, bringing to a simmer.
3. In a separate bowl, mix the flour, baking powder, salt, and milk to make the dumpling dough.
4. Drop spoonfuls of the dough into the simmering soup. Cover and cook for 10-12 minutes, until the dumplings are cooked through.
5. Stir in the shredded chicken, cook for an additional 5 minutes, and serve hot.

Green Curry Vegetables

Ingredients:

- **2 tablespoons olive oil**
- **1 onion**, chopped
- **3 garlic cloves**, minced
- **1 tablespoon grated ginger**
- **1 tablespoon green curry paste**
- **1 can (14 oz) coconut milk**
- **1 cup vegetable broth**
- **2 cups mixed vegetables** (such as bell peppers, zucchini, and carrots)
- **1 tablespoon soy sauce**
- **Salt and pepper**, to taste
- **Fresh cilantro**, for garnish

Instructions:

1. Heat olive oil in a large skillet over medium heat. Add the onion, garlic, and ginger, cooking for 3-4 minutes until softened.
2. Stir in the green curry paste and cook for another minute.
3. Pour in the coconut milk, vegetable broth, and soy sauce, stirring to combine. Bring to a simmer.
4. Add the mixed vegetables and cook for 10-12 minutes, until the vegetables are tender.
5. Season with salt and pepper, and garnish with fresh cilantro before serving.

Stuffed Bell Pepper Casserole

Ingredients:

- **4 bell peppers**, chopped
- **1 lb ground beef**
- **1 onion**, chopped
- **2 garlic cloves**, minced
- **1 cup cooked rice**
- **1 can (14.5 oz) diced tomatoes**
- **1 teaspoon dried oregano**
- **1/2 teaspoon cumin**
- **1/2 cup shredded mozzarella cheese**
- **Salt and pepper**, to taste

Instructions:

1. Preheat the oven to 375°F (190°C). In a large skillet, cook the ground beef, onion, and garlic over medium heat until the beef is browned.
2. Stir in the cooked rice, diced tomatoes, oregano, cumin, salt, and pepper. Cook for 5 minutes, until heated through.
3. Transfer the mixture to a baking dish and sprinkle with shredded mozzarella cheese.
4. Cover with foil and bake for 20 minutes. Remove the foil and bake for an additional 10 minutes, until the cheese is melted and bubbly.

Pork and Cabbage Stir-Fry

Ingredients:

- **1 lb pork tenderloin**, thinly sliced
- **2 tablespoons soy sauce**
- **1 tablespoon sesame oil**
- **1 onion**, sliced
- **1/2 head cabbage**, shredded
- **2 carrots**, julienned
- **2 garlic cloves**, minced
- **1 tablespoon rice vinegar**
- **1 tablespoon hoisin sauce**
- **Sesame seeds**, for garnish

Instructions:

1. Heat sesame oil in a large skillet or wok over medium-high heat. Add the pork and cook for 3-4 minutes until browned.
2. Stir in the onion, cabbage, carrots, and garlic, cooking for another 5 minutes until the vegetables are tender.
3. Add the soy sauce, rice vinegar, and hoisin sauce, stirring to coat. Cook for an additional 2-3 minutes.
4. Garnish with sesame seeds and serve hot.

BBQ Chicken and Cornbread Casserole

Ingredients:

- **4 cooked chicken breasts**, shredded
- **1 can (15 oz) corn kernels**, drained
- **1 cup BBQ sauce**
- **1 box cornbread mix**
- **1/2 cup milk**
- **1 egg**
- **1/2 cup shredded cheddar cheese**
- **Salt and pepper**, to taste

Instructions:

1. Preheat the oven to 375°F (190°C). In a bowl, combine the shredded chicken, corn, and BBQ sauce. Spread the mixture in the bottom of a baking dish.
2. Prepare the cornbread mix according to package instructions, adding the milk and egg. Pour the cornbread batter over the chicken mixture.
3. Bake for 25-30 minutes, or until the cornbread is golden brown and cooked through.
4. Top with shredded cheddar cheese and bake for an additional 5 minutes, until the cheese is melted.

One-Pot Paella

Ingredients:

- 2 tablespoons olive oil
- 1 onion, chopped
- 3 garlic cloves, minced
- 1 red bell pepper, chopped
- 1 cup Arborio rice
- 1/2 teaspoon paprika
- 1/4 teaspoon saffron threads (optional)
- 2 cups chicken broth
- 1 can (14.5 oz) diced tomatoes
- 1/2 cup frozen peas
- 1/2 cup cooked shrimp (optional)
- 1/2 cup cooked chicken, shredded
- 1/4 cup fresh parsley, chopped
- Salt and pepper, to taste
- Lemon wedges, for serving

Instructions:

1. Heat olive oil in a large pot over medium heat. Add the onion, garlic, and bell pepper, cooking for 5-7 minutes until softened.
2. Stir in the Arborio rice, paprika, and saffron (if using), and cook for 2 minutes to toast the rice slightly.
3. Add the chicken broth, diced tomatoes, and peas. Bring to a boil, then reduce to a simmer and cover. Cook for 15-20 minutes, until the rice is tender and the liquid is absorbed.
4. Stir in the shrimp, chicken, and fresh parsley. Season with salt and pepper.
5. Serve with lemon wedges on the side.

Spinach Feta Orzo

Ingredients:

- **1 tablespoon olive oil**
- **1 onion**, chopped
- **2 garlic cloves**, minced
- **2 cups fresh spinach**
- **1 1/2 cups orzo pasta**
- **3 cups vegetable broth**
- **1/2 cup feta cheese**, crumbled
- **1 tablespoon fresh lemon juice**
- **Salt and pepper**, to taste

Instructions:

1. Heat olive oil in a large skillet over medium heat. Add the onion and garlic, cooking for 3-4 minutes until softened.
2. Add the spinach and cook until wilted, about 2-3 minutes.
3. Stir in the orzo pasta and vegetable broth. Bring to a boil, then reduce to a simmer. Cook for 10-12 minutes, stirring occasionally, until the orzo is tender and most of the liquid is absorbed.
4. Stir in the feta cheese and lemon juice. Season with salt and pepper to taste.
5. Serve warm.

Ham and Cheese Macaroni Bake

Ingredients:

- **2 cups elbow macaroni**, cooked
- **2 tablespoons butter**
- **1 onion**, chopped
- **2 garlic cloves**, minced
- **2 cups cooked ham**, cubed
- **2 cups shredded cheddar cheese**
- **1/2 cup grated Parmesan cheese**
- **1 1/2 cups milk**
- **2 tablespoons flour**
- **1 teaspoon mustard powder**
- **1/2 teaspoon paprika**
- **Salt and pepper**, to taste

Instructions:

1. Preheat the oven to 375°F (190°C). In a saucepan, melt butter over medium heat. Add the onion and garlic, cooking for 3-4 minutes until softened.
2. Stir in the flour, mustard powder, and paprika, cooking for 1 minute.
3. Slowly whisk in the milk and bring to a simmer, stirring until the sauce thickens.
4. Stir in the cheddar and Parmesan cheese until melted. Add the cooked ham, macaroni, salt, and pepper.
5. Transfer the mixture to a greased baking dish and bake for 20-25 minutes, until the top is golden and bubbly.

Saffron Chicken and Rice

Ingredients:

- **2 tablespoons olive oil**
- **4 chicken thighs**, skin-on
- **1 onion**, chopped
- **2 garlic cloves**, minced
- **1/2 teaspoon turmeric**
- **1/4 teaspoon saffron threads**, soaked in 2 tablespoons warm water
- **1 1/2 cups long-grain rice**
- **3 cups chicken broth**
- **1/2 cup frozen peas**
- **1/4 cup fresh parsley**, chopped
- **Salt and pepper**, to taste

Instructions:

1. Heat olive oil in a large skillet over medium-high heat. Season the chicken thighs with salt and pepper, then sear the chicken for 5-7 minutes on each side until browned. Remove and set aside.
2. In the same skillet, add the onion and garlic, cooking for 3-4 minutes until softened.
3. Stir in the turmeric and saffron (with its soaking water). Add the rice and cook for 2 minutes, allowing the rice to lightly toast.
4. Pour in the chicken broth and bring to a boil. Reduce the heat to low, return the chicken to the skillet, and cover. Simmer for 20-25 minutes, until the rice is tender and the chicken is cooked through.
5. Stir in the peas and parsley, and season with salt and pepper to taste. Serve warm.

Thai Red Curry with Tofu

Ingredients:

- 2 tablespoons vegetable oil
- **1 onion**, chopped
- **2 garlic cloves**, minced
- **1 tablespoon grated ginger**
- **2 tablespoons red curry paste**
- **1 can (14 oz) coconut milk**
- **1 cup vegetable broth**
- **1 block (14 oz) firm tofu**, cubed
- **1 bell pepper**, sliced
- **1 zucchini**, sliced
- **1 tablespoon soy sauce**
- **1 tablespoon brown sugar**
- **Fresh basil**, for garnish
- **Lime wedges**, for serving

Instructions:

1. Heat vegetable oil in a large skillet or wok over medium heat. Add the onion, garlic, and ginger, cooking for 3-4 minutes until softened.
2. Stir in the red curry paste and cook for 1 minute, until fragrant.
3. Add the coconut milk, vegetable broth, soy sauce, and brown sugar. Bring to a simmer.
4. Stir in the tofu, bell pepper, and zucchini, cooking for 8-10 minutes, until the vegetables are tender.
5. Garnish with fresh basil and serve with lime wedges.

Creamy Chicken Wild Rice Soup

Ingredients:

- **2 tablespoons butter**
- **1 onion**, chopped
- **2 garlic cloves**, minced
- **2 carrots**, diced
- **2 celery stalks**, diced
- **2 cups cooked chicken**, shredded
- **1 cup wild rice**, cooked
- **4 cups chicken broth**
- **1 1/2 cups heavy cream**
- **1 teaspoon thyme**
- **Salt and pepper**, to taste

Instructions:

1. In a large pot, melt butter over medium heat. Add the onion, garlic, carrots, and celery, cooking for 5-7 minutes until softened.
2. Stir in the cooked chicken, wild rice, chicken broth, and thyme. Bring to a simmer and cook for 10 minutes.
3. Stir in the heavy cream, then season with salt and pepper to taste. Simmer for an additional 5-7 minutes, until the soup is creamy and heated through.
4. Serve hot.

Sweet and Sour Pork Stir-Fry

Ingredients:

- **1 lb pork tenderloin**, thinly sliced
- **2 tablespoons soy sauce**
- **1 tablespoon rice vinegar**
- **2 tablespoons sugar**
- **1 tablespoon ketchup**
- **1/2 cup bell peppers**, sliced
- **1/2 cup onions**, sliced
- **1/2 cup pineapple chunks**
- **1 tablespoon vegetable oil**
- **Salt and pepper**, to taste

Instructions:

1. In a small bowl, whisk together soy sauce, rice vinegar, sugar, and ketchup to make the sweet and sour sauce. Set aside.
2. Heat vegetable oil in a large skillet over medium-high heat. Add the pork and cook for 5-7 minutes until browned. Remove from the skillet and set aside.
3. In the same skillet, add the bell peppers, onions, and pineapple. Cook for 3-4 minutes until the vegetables are tender.
4. Return the pork to the skillet and pour in the sweet and sour sauce. Stir to coat everything evenly.
5. Cook for an additional 3-5 minutes, until the sauce thickens. Season with salt and pepper, then serve hot.

Beef and Barley Soup

Ingredients:

- 1 tablespoon olive oil
- **1 lb beef stew meat**, cubed
- **1 onion**, chopped
- **2 garlic cloves**, minced
- **2 carrots**, diced
- **2 celery stalks**, diced
- 1 cup barley
- 4 cups beef broth
- 1 can (14.5 oz) diced tomatoes
- 1 teaspoon thyme
- 1 bay leaf
- **Salt and pepper**, to taste

Instructions:

1. Heat olive oil in a large pot over medium-high heat. Add the beef stew meat and brown on all sides. Remove and set aside.
2. In the same pot, add the onion, garlic, carrots, and celery, cooking for 5-7 minutes until softened.
3. Add the barley, beef broth, diced tomatoes, thyme, and bay leaf. Stir to combine.
4. Return the beef to the pot and bring to a boil. Reduce to a simmer and cook for 45-60 minutes, until the barley is tender and the beef is cooked through.
5. Remove the bay leaf, season with salt and pepper, and serve hot.

Vegetable Lo Mein

Ingredients:

- 8 oz lo mein noodles
- 1 tablespoon sesame oil
- 2 garlic cloves, minced
- 1 carrot, julienned
- 1 bell pepper, thinly sliced
- 1 zucchini, thinly sliced
- 1 cup broccoli florets
- 1/4 cup soy sauce
- 1 tablespoon oyster sauce
- 1 tablespoon hoisin sauce
- 1 teaspoon sugar
- 1/2 teaspoon red pepper flakes (optional)
- 2 green onions, chopped

Instructions:

1. Cook the lo mein noodles according to package instructions. Drain and set aside.
2. Heat sesame oil in a large skillet or wok over medium-high heat. Add the garlic and cook for 1 minute, until fragrant.
3. Add the carrots, bell pepper, zucchini, and broccoli. Stir-fry for 5-7 minutes, until the vegetables are tender-crisp.
4. In a small bowl, whisk together soy sauce, oyster sauce, hoisin sauce, sugar, and red pepper flakes.
5. Add the cooked noodles to the skillet with the vegetables, then pour the sauce over the top. Toss to combine and heat through.
6. Garnish with green onions and serve warm.

Seafood Gumbo

Ingredients:

- 2 tablespoons vegetable oil
- 1/2 cup flour
- **1 onion**, chopped
- **1 bell pepper**, chopped
- **2 celery stalks**, chopped
- **3 garlic cloves**, minced
- 1 can (14.5 oz) diced tomatoes
- 3 cups seafood stock
- 1 teaspoon thyme
- 1/2 teaspoon smoked paprika
- 1 bay leaf
- **1/2 lb shrimp**, peeled and deveined
- 1/2 lb crab meat
- **1/2 lb fish fillets**, cut into pieces (such as cod or tilapia)
- **Salt and pepper**, to taste
- **Fresh parsley**, chopped for garnish

Instructions:

1. In a large pot, heat vegetable oil over medium heat. Whisk in flour and cook, stirring constantly, for about 5 minutes, until the mixture turns a deep golden brown (this is your roux).
2. Add the onion, bell pepper, celery, and garlic. Cook for 5-7 minutes until the vegetables are softened.
3. Stir in the diced tomatoes, seafood stock, thyme, smoked paprika, and bay leaf. Bring to a simmer and cook for 20 minutes.
4. Add the shrimp, crab meat, and fish. Cook for 5-7 minutes, until the seafood is cooked through.
5. Remove the bay leaf, season with salt and pepper, and garnish with fresh parsley.
6. Serve hot over rice, if desired.

Rustic Tuscan Bean Soup

Ingredients:

- **2 tablespoons olive oil**
- **1 onion**, chopped
- **2 garlic cloves**, minced
- **2 carrots**, diced
- **2 celery stalks**, diced
- **1 can (15 oz) white beans**, drained and rinsed
- **1 can (14.5 oz) diced tomatoes**
- **4 cups vegetable broth**
- **1 teaspoon rosemary**
- **1/2 teaspoon thyme**
- **2 cups kale**, chopped
- **Salt and pepper**, to taste

Instructions:

1. Heat olive oil in a large pot over medium heat. Add the onion, garlic, carrots, and celery, cooking for 5-7 minutes until softened.
2. Stir in the white beans, diced tomatoes, vegetable broth, rosemary, and thyme. Bring to a simmer and cook for 15-20 minutes.
3. Add the kale and cook for another 5-7 minutes, until the kale is tender.
4. Season with salt and pepper, and serve hot.

One-Pan Breakfast Hash

Ingredients:

- **2 tablespoons olive oil**
- **1 onion**, chopped
- **2 garlic cloves**, minced
- **2 large potatoes**, diced
- **1 red bell pepper**, chopped
- **1 zucchini**, chopped
- **4 large eggs**
- **Salt and pepper**, to taste
- **Fresh parsley**, chopped for garnish

Instructions:

1. Heat olive oil in a large skillet over medium heat. Add the onion and garlic, cooking for 2-3 minutes until softened.
2. Add the diced potatoes and cook for 10-12 minutes, stirring occasionally, until they begin to soften.
3. Stir in the bell pepper and zucchini, and cook for an additional 5-7 minutes until the vegetables are tender.
4. Create four small wells in the mixture and crack an egg into each. Cover the skillet and cook for 5-7 minutes, until the eggs are cooked to your liking.
5. Season with salt and pepper, then garnish with fresh parsley. Serve hot.

Cheeseburger Casserole

Ingredients:

- **1 lb ground beef**
- **1 onion**, chopped
- **2 garlic cloves**, minced
- **1 can (15 oz) diced tomatoes**
- **1 cup ketchup**
- **1 tablespoon mustard**
- **1/2 teaspoon paprika**
- **2 cups cooked elbow macaroni**
- **2 cups shredded cheddar cheese**
- **Salt and pepper**, to taste

Instructions:

1. Preheat the oven to 375°F (190°C). In a large skillet, cook the ground beef over medium heat until browned. Drain excess fat.
2. Add the onion and garlic, cooking for 3-4 minutes until softened.
3. Stir in the diced tomatoes, ketchup, mustard, paprika, and cooked macaroni. Mix to combine.
4. Transfer the mixture to a greased baking dish and top with shredded cheddar cheese.
5. Bake for 20-25 minutes, until the cheese is melted and bubbly.
6. Serve hot.

www.ingramcontent.com/pod-product-compliance
Lightning Source LLC
LaVergne TN
LVHW081342060526
838201LV00055B/2810